Sisters
Bible Study for Women

Unfailing Love

Growing Closer to Jesus Christ

Participant's Workbook

Rebecca Laird

Abingdon Press / Nashville

Library of Congress Cataloging-in-Publication Data

Laird, Rebecca.
  Unfailing love : growing closer to Jesus Christ : participant's
workbook / Rebecca Laird.
     p. cm.
  ISBN 0-687-00103-X (binding: adhesive : alk. paper)
  1. Christian women—Religious life. I. Title.

  BV4527.L27 2004
  248.8'43—dc22

                                                            2003024821

Scripture quotations from New Revised Standard Version of the Bible, copyright 1989, Division of Christian Education of the National Council of Churches of Christ in the United States of America. Used by permission. All rights reserved.

Scripture taken from *THE MESSAGE.* Copyright © Eugene H. Peterson, 1993, 1994,1995. Used by permission of NavPress Publishing Group.

04 05 06 07 08 09 10 11 12 13—10 9 8 7 6 5 4 3 2 1
MANUFACTURED IN THE UNITED STATES OF AMERICA

For my sisters in the Spirit:

Christine Anderson, Beth Kujan, Lisa Matthews,

Sarah White, and Julie Yarborough

Contents

Introduction

Friendship is a word that evokes images of times spent with someone we enjoy. Friendship can be based on mutual interests, memorable times, or just that great energy that radiates from people whose hearts beat at a similar rate. As we become friends with someone, we slowly let down our guard and begin to be fully ourselves in each other's presence. We begin as acquaintances; then as trust grows, we begin to understand and depend upon each other more. Friends also learn to take some risks with each other, to let their wounded and broken places show. In this kind of relationship, healing and vulnerability, compassion and forgiveness not only are possible but necessary. Such a relationship awaits us with Jesus Christ.

Thinking of Jesus as a friend may be a new idea to you, but it is Jesus' idea to consider us his friends. In the Gospel of John, Jesus says to his disciples—those with whom he spent his time teaching, eating, and serving side by side—"No one has greater love than this, to lay down one's life for one's friends. You are my friends if you do what I command you. I do not call you servants any longer because the servant does not know what the master is doing; but I have called you friends, because I have made known to you everything that I have heard from my Father" (15:13-15).

Jesus calls us to friendship with him and friendship with those who also seek to follow his commands and call on their lives. But what is a friend? A *friend* by definition is someone who is intimate with and fond of you. A *friend* is one who is on the same side in the struggle of life. It is very good news to know that Jesus is fond of us and is pulling for each one of us in the difficulties of our own lives.

UNFAILING LOVE has been designed to help you grow closer to Jesus. As with any friendship, we start by getting to know each other. An intimate friendship cannot be forced, but it can be formed with bonds of great love over time. Your job, then, is to come just as you are with your desire to know Jesus as a reliable and loving friend who can walk with you and talk with you on the deepest spiritual level.

HOW FRIENDSHIP DEVELOPS

When we first meet someone, our first hours together are spent learning some details of each other's lives. Where were you born? Tell me about your mom and dad and your siblings. What life events shaped you or set you on your life's course? What are your hopes and dreams? What makes you happy? What do you like to do? What just "gets to you"? In time, we will hear family stories. We may page through old photo albums to see what the person looked like in earlier years. We spend time together. Sometimes we are face to face; other times we stay in touch despite physical distances. Our shared time and cumulative knowledge grow until we feel comfortable and fully accepted in the other's presence. We begin to trust that we are understood and not alone in the world. Someone else values us and wants to share with us what is important to her and will listen to us in return. That is a real friendship.

HOW THIS BOOK IS DESIGNED

The goal of UNFAILING LOVE is to help you develop a spiritual friendship with Jesus. Each week's lesson will focus on a specific story or aspect of Jesus' life. *Week One* will focus on the birth and early life of Jesus. *Week Two* will help us understand how Jesus' spiritual identity was shaped and tested at his baptism in the Jordan. *Week Three* will look at the way Jesus healed and loved others. *Week Four* will focus on Jesus' instructions to his closest disciples. *Week Five* will follow Jesus to the cross, and *Week Six* will take us through the hope of the Resurrection.

The material for each week begins with an introduction of the week's theme. Then for four days there are daily readings, each of which is followed by reflection questions, with space to write your responses. *Day One* provides a window into the theme for the week through a personal story. *Day Two* provides introductory comments concerning Jesus and a reading of the Scripture passage that we will focus on for the rest of the week. *Day Three* offers background to the Scripture to help us understand its spiritual meanings. *Day Four* helps us see what the passage reveals about the person and character of Jesus. *Day Five* will help us live the Scripture rather than just read it.

On *Day Six* of each week, you will be asked to spend your time praying a psalm. Remember that good first-century Jews like Jesus knew and prayed the Psalms, and this knowledge shows throughout the Gospels. To love Jesus is to pray as he did. You will find more instructions on how to pray the Psalms in Week One.

On *Day Seven* you will meet with your group. In preparation for your meeting, take some sabbath, restful time. Go for a walk. Take a catnap. Write a letter to someone you miss. Do the things that make life meaningful. After all, Jesus told us that he came that we might have abundant life. Taking time both to savor quiet times and serve others helps us to live abundant lives, and that was Jesus' ideal.

LUKE: OUR BASIC RESOURCE

All of the stories about Jesus in this study are from the Gospel of Luke. This Gospel was written as a clear account of the life of Jesus for "Theophilus," a name that literally means "friend of God" or "dear to God." Luke offers us an "orderly account" of Jesus' life that shows him as a man of prayer and action. Moreover, Luke's Gospel has some special material that is not found in the other Gospels. For example, Luke is where we find the stories about Jesus' birth and infancy. Conversely, Mark, the Gospel many think was written first, tells us nothing about Jesus' birth or resurrection. Although Matthew has no mention of a stable, it does tell of the wise men. Mark and John introduce Jesus at the beginning of his public ministry. In addition, Luke recounts stories of healings and some parables that are not found in the other Gospels.

Finally, Luke details the Resurrection and the days after in greater detail than do the other Gospels and then describes Jesus' ascension into heaven. Mark does not mention the Resurrection, and Matthew does not describe the Ascension. The Gospels emphasize different characteristics and details in the life of Jesus. Luke gives the most complete picture of Jesus' historical life.

Many biblical scholars believe that the Gospel of Luke was written by a second- or third-generation Christian who studied the existing written narratives about Jesus, like Mark, and also talked to those who knew the eyewitnesses who had followed Jesus. From these sources, the Gospel was written to help believers then and now understand how Jesus brought God's love to earth and drew all sorts of people of God—male and female, Jew and Gentile—toward heaven. The Gospel of Luke shows Jesus' special interest in women and the poor and how Jesus followed a pattern of active ministry and solitary prayer. Luke shows us that Jesus was a son, student, teacher, healer, boundary-breaker, friend to many, and risen Lord. This is the Jesus Luke describes. This is the Jesus we will learn to love more deeply and come to trust as our beloved friend.

Through these weeks, we begin to understand what Jesus meant when he said, "You are my friends if you do what I command you. . . . I have made known to you everything that I have heard from my father" (John 15:14-15). We will discover that each of Jesus' commands and teachings is rooted in his unfailing love for us and for the world. We are being asked to listen carefully to discover who Jesus is and what Jesus taught. What Jesus has learned from God he is passing on to us, his spiritual friends.

Week One:
A Child Born
to High Expectations

DAY ONE: CHALLENGING EXPECTATIONS

Readings for the Week: Luke 1–2; Psalm 111

When our trail guides spoke the words "French Lake" to our group of eight hot, tired, bug-bitten backpackers who had been hiking in California's High Sierras for several days, we all imagined an oasis awaiting us at day's end. If we followed our terrain map and stuck together, not leaving anyone to lag behind on the steep trail, our guides agreed to go ahead to prepare a special meal and campsite for us.

The day's journey looked clear on the map, but the ground we trod proved challenging. Riverbeds that marked the easiest route had dried up. What looked like steady inclines on the map turned out to be rocky faces for us to scale. To make matters worse, the guides appointed me and one other person to be the map readers and trail leaders. The two of us were capable leaders but novice backpackers. The more experienced campers had been required to follow our lead, no matter where we led them.

For hours we shuffled along under the summer sun making slow and uneven progress. By nightfall we found the final ledge that would take us to French Lake. Spirits began to soar, and energy surged anew. Expectations were high. We could almost taste the food waiting for us and feel the cool waters of the lake on our parched faces. We rounded the final bend, and indeed our guides were there waiting for us. But behind them was a deep river ravine with a rope and bucket contraption rigged as a bridge to transport us across the abyss to French Lake.

I stopped in my tracks. No way was I going to hang from a makeshift rope bridge high above a river when I was bone tired! I was *not* going to do this. I balked. This was not what I was expecting at all.

Several others stepped forward and were secured onto the rope bridge with their backpacks. With a huge push from the guide on our side of the ravine, they swung their legs as instructed to propel themselves across the ravine to where a second guide unbuckled them and welcomed them to the dinner party with warm food and fresh fruit. Every fiber of my being was in rebellion. No way was this right. I'd done what I'd been asked to do. I'd put one foot in front of the other all day long, and now I was being asked to trust in a way I never imagined.

Eventually, I had no choice. I would be left alone on one side of the ravine, or I would trust that my guides knew what they were doing. I allowed myself to be strapped on; and before I knew it, I was hanging in mid-air over a rushing river. I swung my legs for as long as I could; but several dozen feet from the other side, I simply ran out of energy.

"Pull me in. Please pull me in," I called to the guide who held my safety rope. Thinking I was giving up, he refused. My husband, who had crossed before me, stepped up saying, "She's not a quitter. She really must need help."

They pulled me in, and my feet touched solid ground. Once I was unhooked, I stumbled to the campsite, deposited my backpack, and bit into a piece of fresh pineapple. Within minutes, I had peeled off my socks and was wading in the cool waters of French Lake.

The promise of French Lake was finally fulfilled, but not without challenging all my expectations about how we would get there and what it would take from me.

The first-century Jews were awaiting a messiah. They thought they knew who they were looking for and how he would save them as a conquering king; but then Jesus came, not as a king but as a baby with no home and born to parents who were unmarried. No way. This couldn't be God's best plan, but indeed it was. The promise was fulfilled, but not without challenging their expectations and asking them to trust God in ways they could not have imagined.

Reflecting and Recording

1. What expectations do you have of someone who promises to guide you and be your friend?

2. What expectations do you have of Jesus? Write several words or phrases that describe how you expect Jesus to act on behalf of his friends.

3. When has your faith challenged your expectations? Have you ever expected Jesus to answer your prayers in ways that did not come to pass? Have your prayers been answered in unexpected ways?

4. If Jesus were to come again tomorrow, how would you expect him to come? What would you expect him to do and be?

DAY TWO: BORN TO SAVE

The Gospel of Luke opens with background information that places the events of Jesus' birth into the larger picture of great expectations held by the first-century Jews. In the first verse of the Gospel, Luke tells us that he will write "an orderly account of the events that have been fulfilled among us." He retraces the ways God's promises unfolded.

The first two chapters of Luke announce the births of John the Baptist and Jesus, two boys sent by God for special purposes to an extended prayerful family. These parallel birth stories show how God foretells and is active in both births. We learn early that God will bring about salvation through these two, with one being sent to prepare the way for the second, who is to reign as king forever.

First, John was born under special circumstances. The angel Gabriel visited Zechariah, a faithful priest who would become John's father, with the news of John's impending birth. When his wife Elizabeth conceived, she realized God's activity in her life. Soon the angel Gabriel made another visit, this one to Mary, a young relative of Elizabeth. After Mary struggled with her fear and questions, she magnified the Lord and said yes to God's miraculous plan. The parallel stories work together in Luke to announce God's plan to fulfill God's promises to send an heir to fill the long-empty throne of King David.

In Chapter 2 we learn that Jesus' birth, while humble in circumstances, was announced in the heavens and recognized by lowly shepherds. At

Jesus' circumcision, Simeon and Anna, two devout people, recognized the baby Jesus as the long-awaited redeemer of Israel. (As an important side note, Simeon prophesied that Jesus had also come to be a light of revelation to the Gentiles, those who are non-Jews. This was the first indication that Jesus had come for all people.) Surrounded by his family, Jesus grew and eventually made the annual pilgrimage to Jerusalem, where he not only learned from his teachers but became as an equal to them, as one who answered questions.

A key theme in these first chapters is, *Who is this highly expected child, and why has he come?*

Spend the remaining time you have today reading the first two chapters of Luke. Read both chapters. It is often helpful to read aloud. Scripture was written to be spoken. You may notice something new in these familiar passages as you say the words as well as read them.

Reflecting and Recording

1. What do these chapters tell us about the extended family of Jesus? What kind of people did God choose to be Jesus' closest kin?

2. Why do you think that Zechariah, Elizabeth, Mary, Simeon, and Anna all reacted to the news of God's activity with praise? What other responses did they show?

3. These chapters tell us of angels appearing. They tell of the Holy Spirit filling Elizabeth, coming upon Mary, and later resting on Simeon. What did the angel do and say? What did the Holy Spirit do? Do you believe angels speak today? Does the Holy Spirit act? Why or why not?

DAY THREE: A YES ATTITUDE

If you are going to spend your life with someone in an intimate spiritual friendship, it's a good idea to meet his mother. The first chapter of Luke shows us the spiritual sensitivity of Jesus' mother and the religious expectancy shared by his extended family. Jesus' family did not know exactly what God might do, but they trusted that God would indeed fulfill the promises to their people. Let's look today at the attitude of expectancy and availability that surrounded Jesus' birth.

Zechariah and Elizabeth recognized God's activity at Jesus' birth because they had spent years waiting in expectation for God to act. The Bible tells us that when Elizabeth greeted Mary, she said, "Blessed are you among women. . . . Blessed is she who believed that there would be a fulfillment of what was spoken to her by the Lord" (1:42, 45). Mary, while very young, willingly walked forward into unknown circumstances, confident that God was with her.

The familiar words from Mary's song of praise proclaimed her faith in a God who had just turned her life upside-down. These words expressed her faith in a God who had done great things for her in the past. She assumed God would continue to act on her behalf as she stepped forward to shoulder her wonderful but inexplicable task.

Mary was at a wondrous yet terrifying stage of life. On the one hand, she teetered on the verge of parenthood, knowing that soon a brand new person of great promise would enter the world. On the other hand, she

19

knew she would be the one responsible for rearing this little person; and she would be the one left to worry and pray for decades after.

When Mary said, "Let it be with me according to your word," she did so knowing life would never be the same.

The life of faith requires each of us to take a leap of faith.

Most of us can remember a time when our lives forever changed. For some of us it may have been when we met the person we would marry. Perhaps it was the day we turned from going our way to going God's way.

For me that milestone date in my life was December 1, the date my youngest child was diagnosed with cancer. It was a day that I had to say "yes" and trust that God would walk with me into the terrifying future, a time when I felt ill-prepared to travel an uncertain path to an uncertain future with my five-year-old.

I didn't find it easy to say yes that fateful day or in the years that followed, which brought my daughter's healing. I simply found it necessary. I didn't understand God's ways and certainly would have chosen an easier road. Instead, I trusted that sometimes faith requires a yes through fear, doubt, and tremendous sorrow. The Bible frequently reminds us of that truth.

Whenever God calls us to an unexpected relationship—just as God called Mary to love a miraculous child—we can trust that God is with us before the word *yes* has left our lips and our feet have left the floor to take the first trusting step.

Reflecting and Recording

1. What are you expecting from God? Are you willing to wait and pray like Zechariah, Simeon, and Anna? How might prayer prepare you to see God at work in ways we might otherwise miss?

2. How have you said yes to God in your life?

3. Why do you think God chose Mary to be the mother of Jesus? What qualities does she exhibit? What qualities do you possess that you trust God will find useful?

DAY FOUR: HUMAN AND DIVINE

Yesterday, we looked at the expectations that surrounded Jesus' birth. Today, we see how those closest to him began to understand that the son and young boy they knew was not just Mary's son but the divine son of God.

Jesus and his devoutly Jewish family made an annual pilgrimage to Jerusalem, presumably for Passover. After the seven-day festival ended, the group from Nazareth headed home. At the end of a day's journey, Mary and Joseph looked for Jesus among the group, and he wasn't there. They turned around and went back. Three days later, they found him in the Temple, sitting among the teachers. They were not happy parents at that moment. For several days they had not known where their 12-year-old son was. Mary must have been undone. I recall a day when, due to a carpool snafu, I couldn't find my oldest daughter for 20 minutes. I was panicked. When Mary saw Jesus after three days, she said, "Child, why have you treated us like this? Look, your father and I have been searching for you in great anxiety." To put this in more understandable terms, "Where have you been? We've been worried sick about you!"

Jesus replied with the surety of adolescence: "Why were you searching for me? Did you not know that I must be in my father's house?" Mary didn't understand her son's words.

In *The Message,* Mary's response is paraphrased this way: She "held these things dearly, deep within herself."

Then slowly and surely Mary began to see Jesus' life and, no doubt, hers from a different angle. Her worldview had been jarred, her everyday priorities and plans were no longer the same. She must have been concerned with Jesus' safety, health, and happiness, as mothers are. However, when confronted with the wonder of it all, when thrust into God's bigger yet baffling picture of life, she chose to hold these things deeply within her—in the place of transformation.

This baby that Mary bore and raised was more than the infant she rocked or the child she comforted and encouraged. In him was mystery. In him was wonder. In him was a mixture of divinity and humanity. The only way to understand such things is to ponder them deeply and long, where God's work of transformation and wisdom takes place. When faced with the extraordinary things of God, we are asked to put aside hasty affirmations or quick questions and remain open to the unexpected ways of God.

Luke shows us throughout these first two chapters that Jesus is both God and human, which is what is meant by the word *incarnation*. Luke tells us that Mary is Jesus' mother. (She is referred to as the *theotokos* or "God bearer" by Orthodox Christians.) From her Jesus receives his humanity. His "God-genes" come directly by the action of the Holy Spirit. Who can understand how God can become incarnate and how a human being can be fully one with God? It is one of those mysteries that we affirm and must ponder in our hearts.

At his circumcision Jesus was taken to the Temple. In Jewish understanding the Temple is where the divine and human meet through ritual and sacrifice. In his youth, Jesus returned to the Temple to learn of the things of God, and he amazed his teachers. Clearly he was born to his task. Luke wants us to understand that Jesus is God's long-awaited one, who has come to reunite heaven and earth (God and humanity) in his very body and by his divine wisdom.

We are not the first ones to struggle with the idea of how Jesus could be both human and divine. The early church also had differing opinions. In the fourth century, a church leader named Arius argued that Jesus was special but not divine. Athanasius, another church leader, countered that

Jesus was thoroughly divine and must be in order to redeem humanity. Others argued that Jesus was not really human but only appeared to be. By the year 325, the emperor Constantine, who had converted to Christianity, convened important Christian leaders at the Council of Nicea to settle the debate. They affirmed that Jesus was "one in being" and "one in substance" with God. That is why when we recite the Nicene Creed, we say, "We believe in one Lord, Jesus Christ," who is "true God from true God, begotten, not made, of one Being with the Father."

Reflecting and Recording

1. Looking back can you see your life from a wider angle? Can you see God at work in times when you thought God was absent or silent?

2. How do you understand Jesus as fully human and fully God? Where would you find yourself in the debate over how Jesus could be both human and divine?

3. Faith requires an ability to believe when things are beyond our human understanding. Is this easy or hard for you?

DAY FIVE: PROMISES AND PRAISES

Three times in the first two chapters of Luke God fulfilled promises. Zechariah prayed for his wife Elizabeth to bear a son, and she did. Zechariah responded by praising God and saying: "Blessed be the Lord God of Israel / for he has looked favorably on his people and redeemed them. . . . / [God] has remembered his holy covenant" (1:68, 72). Zechariah understood his own blessing was related to God's ongoing covenant with all of the people of Israel.

Unsuspecting Mary received a promise that she would bear a son, and she was to name him Jesus. In response to being God's unexpected chosen one, Mary sang, "My soul magnifies the Lord, / and my spirit rejoices in God my Savior" (1:47). She linked her good favor with the mercy and might God shows to the lowly and hungry.

Simeon clung to a promise made by the Holy Spirit that he would live to see the Messiah; and when Jesus was brought to the Temple, he recognized Jesus as the Messiah. He raised his arms and praised God saying, "My eyes have seen your salvation, / which you have prepared in the presence of all peoples" (2:30-31). Simeon knew that the gift he received in seeing Jesus with his own eyes was not just personal good fortune. He understood his role in identifying the special role Jesus would fulfill.

The pattern is clear: God promises to deliver and act. God keeps these promises in ways and at times we cannot predict. Our task is to wait with expectancy and be quick to offer praise when God's activity breaks through.

Years ago, the inner-city church I attended helped start an emergency shelter for homeless families. It became the first stop for families in crisis. As Christmas approached, the money to keep the shelter running was scarce. Some grant money had been promised, but we had not yet received it. We wondered if we would have to shut down before the holiday. It didn't seem wise to keep running without adequate funds. The board of directors held various views, until one member spoke up and asked: "But what if Mary comes to us on Christmas? What if there is a single mom out there with nowhere to go on Christmas?" The shelter stayed open. Late on Christmas Eve, a woman with a young baby knocked on the door looking for a place to sleep. The amazed staff marveled and praised God that the doors were still open. The shelter was full, and there were no empty cribs. The staff simply lined with blankets a shopping cart that had been left outside and made a snug bed for the baby, which was rolled next to the mother's bed.

On Christmas Day, our church rejoiced. We had trusted God's promises to provide, and our only response was absolute praise.

Reflecting and Recording

1. Both Zechariah and Mary showed that they understood that God's blessing was not given only for personal happiness but also for the betterment of others. How have God's blessings to you allowed you to share the blessings with others?

2. Simeon made a public proclamation of praise and prophecy about Jesus in the Temple. Do you most often offer your praises silently or when you are out in public? Why?

3. Have you ever felt like God was using you to be God's answer for someone in need? What happened? What was your response?

DAY SIX: A PSALM OF FAITHFULNESS

To pray a psalm or any part of Scripture, we read it slowly so that it can warm us like spring sunshine thaws the frozen ground. Set aside 10–15 minutes. Begin with a simple prayer asking that God will illumine you and be present with you through your reading of Scripture. Desire a word of love and guidance from God rather than focusing on specific facts to memorize. Read slowly and ponder thoughtfully with a receptive heart. When a word or phrase catches your attention, stop and let the words or images soak in for a moment. Don't hurry on. When you sense a subtle release of attention from the first word or phrase, continue reading. The Psalms were written as poetry and song, so it is beneficial to read them aloud when possible.

Pray Psalm 111. This psalm would have been said during a festival time at the Temple for worship. It could have been prayed during Passover when Jesus and his family went to the Temple. The psalm reaffirms God's faithfulness. It affirms that the best response possible to God's revelation and redemption is praise. Zechariah, Mary, Simeon, and Anna all knew this. We now join them as we pray this psalm.

DAY SEVEN: GROUP MEETING

Prepare for the meeting in quiet, restful activities. Think about what you have learned and what you would like to share. Remember your group members in prayer and prepare yourself to hear what they have to say as well as what God is saying to you.

Week Two:
You Are the Beloved

DAY ONE: WASHED AND PREPARED BY LOVE

Readings for the Week: Luke 3–4:13; Psalm 91

Reverend Susan Gregg-Schroeder tells the story of a Protestant seminary professor who took some students on a tour of Russia. They gathered in a Russian Orthodox Church on the evening before the feast of Epiphany where they were preparing to celebrate Jesus' baptism—one of those moments where Jesus' divine identity was revealed. The night before Epiphany, the celebration was all about water. Great tubs of water were placed all around the grand cathedral. In Orthodox churches, people are free to mill around as hymns and liturgy that emphasize God's gift of water are sung and enacted. Many of the worshipers went to the great basins of water and filled jars and pans they had brought from home.

The students hung back, bewildered by the different sights and the worship style of these fellow Christians. The professor, noticing their response, motioned for them to follow an elderly woman outside to the porch. He asked the woman, "Could you tell us why you were filling that bottle with water and what you will do with it?"

She replied, "Tomorrow my daughter-in-law will bring my first grand-child to the house, and I will give my grandchild a bath. I will mix some of the water from the bottle with the bath water, and then pray to God that as I clean the body of this beautiful child, given to us as a gift, that the Spirit of God will make this child pure and holy, and that God will claim this child as God's own.

"I will then clean our house. Our house is an extension of the church because Christians live in it. It is holy space. I will pour some of the water into the bucket I will use to scrub the house. And I will pray, 'O God, as I clean this house, make it a fit dwelling place for your Holy Spirit so that we may rejoice in your presence among us.'

"And at night, since our tongues and stomachs must enter into this feast, I will make a special soup, an Epiphany soup. And as I mix the water from this bottle I have, I will pray that God might fill our hungry spirits even as God fills our hungry bodies."

Later in the conversation, one of the students asked, "Are you making holy water?"

She answered, "No, we are not making holy water. We are declaring all water holy."

This story beautifully reminds us that the baptismal waters wash us, prepare us, and seal us in God's goodness. In Jesus' life and in ours, our baptism is a starting point for understanding who we are in God's sight.

Reflecting and Recording

1. Do you remember your baptism? (If you were baptized as a baby, perhaps you have seen pictures or heard stories.) Was it a memorable occasion? Why?

2. Different churches practice different modes of baptism. Some baptize children, some only adults. Some sprinkle a little water, while others fully immerse in water. What does your church practice and why?

3. The Russian grandmother in this story makes the point that water is a good gift of creation, and that ordinary water is holy because God made it. Likewise, God made each human child and declared both the water and the human creatures good at creation. God reaffirms this claim in baptism. How does knowing you are created by God and publicly affirmed as a child of God's lasting covenant at baptism have an impact on your sense of spiritual identity?

DAY TWO: SPIRITUAL IDENTITY

The first two chapters of Luke have helped us see how Jesus' birth raised expectations that he was the long-awaited leader who will bring salvation. We turn to the next portion of Luke knowing that high hopes are riding on Jesus. The possibility of change hangs in the air.

Chapter 3 opens by focusing on the ministry of John. His presence and preaching was powerful, and many heeded his call to repentance. Many began to wonder, *Is John the one we've been waiting for?* Then, Jesus joined John at the Jordon River; and the speculation on the identity of the Messiah ended when the Holy Spirit descended like a dove on Jesus after he was baptized. The voice from heaven confirmed it: Jesus is not only the son of God, he is the beloved one of God.

Immediately after establishing Jesus' identity in God, Luke recounts a list of ancestors in Jesus' human family tree. This shows us both that Jesus is God's Son because God has publicly declared it so at his baptism and that Jesus is also God's Son by lineage through his human family tree. (Notice that the genealogy ends with the phrases, "son of Adam, son of God." Either way you look at Jesus, from his divine or human side, he is traceable back to God.)

Then, as soon as we learn exactly who Jesus is, he was led by the Spirit to the wilderness to be tempted. His identity is as God's beloved one, God's agent of redemption; and as such his actions were directed by God through the Holy Spirit. Immediately we are shown that one who is

God's beloved must go where God leads, even if that place happens not to be the place one would desire. In this case, Jesus went to the wilderness to have his newly declared identity as the Son of God sorely tested. Would Jesus stand firm in his understanding of who he is in God's sight? Or would he listen to the devil, ("the slanderer") and claim the power God had granted him for his personal use rather than for God's glory?

Spend the remaining time you have today reading Luke 3–4:13. Read the section at one sitting. It may be helpful to read aloud. Scripture was written to be spoken. You may notice something new in these familiar passages as you say the words aloud.

Reflecting and Recording

1. What determines your identity? When people first meet you, what do you disclose about yourself?

2. What do you think God says about you? Are you the "beloved of God," or is that term just a designation for Jesus?

3. Why would God declare that Jesus is his beloved child and then lead him directly into temptation? Have you ever experienced back-to-back periods of blessing and testing?

DAY THREE: LISTEN WITH GREAT ATTENTIVENESS

The story of Jesus' baptism reflects God's action in the passing of the baton from John to Jesus. John had come to prepare the way and call people to repentance and right moral action. John told the people, who felt oppressed and rendered powerless by the government, to share what they had and to be honest and fair about money and power. John's message was powerful, but he was not saying anything that the Hebrew prophets before him had not said. Indeed, he followed the lead of the earlier prophets in what he said and proclaimed. Many heeded his call and came to be baptized. Just when expectations rose about John's possible role as Messiah, John pointed to Jesus. John was soon imprisoned by Herod, who represented both the oppressive government and those who personally resisted John's moral claims and call to repentance. John was then out of the picture, and Jesus took center stage.

Jesus was dramatically affirmed as God's Son at his baptism; then he was led to the desert, where we can see if Jesus is worthy of the title *Son of God.* A key question in the Temptation story is, Will Jesus use his power for God's purposes or for his own?

This story of Jesus' temptation is Jesus' own personal exodus story. His story shows us that his special identity as God's Beloved is in continuity with the special heritage of the Israelites who were chosen by God (just as he was) and were led to the desert to wander. Jesus knew what happened in the wilderness—he was, after all, a good Jew who knew his Torah.

36

Deuteronomy 8:2, which Jesus would have known by heart, says: "Remember the long way that the LORD your God has led you these forty years in the wilderness, in order to humble you, testing you to know what was in your heart, whether or not you would keep his commandments."

The kind of God who would lead the Israelites and his beloved Son into times of wandering where they would face temptation is the same God who called them to lives of obedience.

According to author Henri Nouwen, "The word 'obedience' comes from the Latin, which means to listen with great attentiveness" (From "Parting Words: A Conversation with Henri Nouwen," an interview by the author for *Sacred Journey, The Journal of Fellowship in Prayer,* December 1996; page 10). Obedience often conjures up the image of a subordinate snapping to attention, but its root offers a different image: one of leaning forward, close to the lips of a loved one, so that you might hear what they want to say specifically to you.

Jesus was lead by the Spirit into the wilderness to learn to listen with great attentiveness to God's design for his public ministry.

Reflecting and Recording

1. Why did John's teaching of repentance and call to right behavior anger Herod? Why does bringing up matters of justice and the right use of money always stir emotions?

2. Do you think Jesus could have used his power for his own purposes rather than for God's purposes? Why is power so easy to misuse?

3. How do you define *obedience*? Is it helpful to think of obedience as listening with great attentiveness to the one who loves you most? Why or why not?

DAY FOUR: TEMPTED TO DOUBT GOD'S LOVE

Each of the temptations Jesus faced tells us something about what it meant for him to be the Son of God. He was tempted to take the fast track and follow in the prescribed leadership roles of his culture. He could be the one to solve all the world's hunger problems. He could be the one to unify the world as a political leader. He could be a miracle worker who wowed the whole world into believing in God. Instead, the temptations show that Jesus' power was to be used in obedience to God through service, even if that meant he would suffer along the way.

The first temptation Jesus faced was to turn stone into bread. The Scripture seems to imply that Jesus was led to the desert where he became hungry after days of fasting. There, in that weakened physical state, the devil (whose name, as I have mentioned, means "the slanderer") stepped up to take advantage of his vulnerability.

Jesus was hungry to the point of death, and the slanderer mocked Jesus. It is as if he was saying. "Yeah, right. God loves you and sent you here to starve to death. If you have the power that was promised, feed yourself, for goodness sake. And feed the world while you are at it."

Jesus listened with great attentiveness and, even in his hunger and desire to alleviate his and the world's suffering, he heard God's instruction. God did not send Jesus and call him Beloved so he could become the village baker or water pump to fulfill every human need. Yes, sometimes he fed, and fed thousands at that, but that was not his sole purpose for coming. He was to be about more than bread. Human need was not to direct his living and giving; obedience to God was to direct his path.

In the second temptation Jesus was offered authority over the entire political world. First-century Palestine was awash with messianic expectations. People were waiting for the Messiah to come and throw the Romans out of office. They wanted the Kingdom of Israel restored under a new king—a descendant of David. Jesus fit the bill.

Under these pressures Jesus listened with great attentiveness and replied, "Worship the Lord your God / and serve only him" (Luke 3:8).

The devil tempted Jesus with being the world's leader and hero. But Jesus listened with great attentiveness and concluded that God's strategy for him was different. This was Jesus' temptation to be relevant in the world's eyes. Jesus chose instead to be obedient to a path of service.

The third temptation strikes at the religious heart of a very religious Jesus. He was a devout, synagogue-attending Jew. The devil took him to Jerusalem and placed him on the pinnacle of the Temple and said, "If you are the Son of God, throw yourself down from here" and let the angels catch you!

The devil quoted from Psalm 91. The psalm says that when the Anointed One comes, the angels will guard him and protect him and not let him even stub his toe. If this Scripture is true, the devil said: "Let's test it in a spectacular way. Prove you are God's beloved in front of all the Jews worshiping in the Temple. Prove it in front of the Temple priests and rabbis. Jump, Jesus! Or don't you believe God will really come through for you?"

This was Jesus' temptation to bring all of the people to faith in a spectacular, high-profile way. Instead, Jesus listened with attentiveness and answered, "God is not to be tested nor proved but obeyed."

Jesus' temptations are uniquely his. We may not be tempted to turn stones to bread, become leader of the world, or become a spectacular religious wonder-worker, but we all are faced with the same essential challenges.

We are all tempted to doubt God's love for us.

We are tempted to turn away from the path of obedience and service and choose instead to be well liked, able to fix the world's ills, or have remarkable faith and spiritual powers.

However, the call is clear: We are called to listen with great attentiveness to God's ongoing declaration that we are loved with an everlasting love through whatever befalls us.

Your task and mine is to listen with great attentiveness and prayer, and God will show us what to say and what to do step by step, day by day, even through the wilderness times.

Reflecting and Recording

1. What are you tempted to believe about God in difficult times? Have you ever doubted God's love, God's power, or God's plan?

2. Are you tempted most by the desire to be well liked, to be able to fix others' problems, or to have great faith and remarkable spiritual powers? Are you tempted by something else?

3. What kind of negative thoughts or doubts could "the slanderer" use to make you doubt God's love? Are there any recurring thoughts that keep you from trusting that you are loved?

DAY FIVE: REMEMBER WHO YOU ARE

Henri Nouwen, one of the great spiritual writers of our time, was a former professor at Yale and Harvard. In the later part of his life he became pastor to a community created to care for mentally disabled persons. He said this passage of the heavens opening is the moment when Jesus' core identity was both revealed to the world and claimed by Jesus. Nouwen writes:

This is the core experience of Jesus. He is reminded in a deep, deep way of who he is. The temptations in the desert are temptations to move him away from that spiritual identity. He was tempted to believe he was someone else. . . ."No, No, No. I am the Beloved from God." I think his whole life is continually claiming that identity in the midst of everything. There are times in which he is praised, times when he is despised or rejected, but he keeps saying, "Others will leave me alone, but my Father will not leave me alone. I am the Beloved Son of God. I am the hope found in that identity."

(From "Parting Words: A Conversation with Henri Nouwen":
an interview by the author for *Sacred Journey:
The Journal of Fellowship in Prayer*, December 1996; page 9)

In the movie, *The Lion King*, Simba, a lion cub, is born to Mufasa, the Lion King. Simba is born knowing he is in line for the throne. The movie's early action centers around Simba's mistaken notion of what it means to be king. He dreams of power and privilege and has to learn that kingly power comes with kingly responsibilities. His power is not to be used for his benefit but is given so that with wise use all creatures who live in the Pridelands will flourish. When Simba resists his kingly responsibilities, he wanders for a while in the wilderness. The turning point comes when his father appears to him in a vision and says: "Remember who you are."

Simba has to come to terms with his heritage and his calling. We all do.

Each of us as children of God claim our identity in baptism. We reaffirm our identity every time we choose God's way (when we are tempted to use money or power or time for purposes other than for God). We reclaim our identity each time we offer the gifts we have to those placed in our care. When we act out of obedience to God's loving claim on our lives and serve his purposes, we are remembering who we truly are. As we respond out of our core identity as God's beloved children, we are transformed more and more into the divine image first implanted in our lives at creation and then redeemed through Christ.

Reflecting and Recording

1. What did your family or others close to you as you were growing up say about who you are? Did they build up your sense of being God's child? Did they tear it down? How do those early influences have an impact on your sense of spiritual identity today?

2. When and where can you best hear the quiet voice of God?

3. Have you ever wandered away from your core identity or responsibilities as God's child? What brought you back?

DAY SIX: A PSALM OF AFFIRMATION

Pray Psalm 91. This psalm is a prayer for and affirmation of God's protection. God's promise of protection, deliverance, and rescue from temptation and harm is sure. Direct allusions to this psalm are found in Luke's story of Jesus' temptation in the wilderness. When we pray this psalm, we know that Jesus also prayed it at times when he was tempted to forget that he was God's beloved child. We can pray it remembering that God's love and provision for us is sure even in times of temptation or difficulty.

DAY SEVEN: GROUP MEETING

Prepare for the meeting in quiet, restful activities. Think about what you have learned and what you would like to share. Remember your group members in prayer and prepare yourself to hear what they have to say as well as what God is saying to you.

Week Three:
Made for a Mission

DAY ONE: LED BY THE SPIRIT

Readings for the Week: Luke 4–9; Psalm 40

Have you ever been led by the Spirit somewhere? I have been aware of such leading a time or two. I absolutely knew after college that I had been led to San Francisco to help start a church for the homeless and urban poor. My parents thought I'd moved to Sodom and would never find a husband. I thought I'd found a little piece of paradise. My skin tingled with the rightness of being there.

But the life wasn't easy. I was very young and very optimistic and aware of God's goodness; but those we sought to serve were not easy people. Most owned next to nothing and needed so much: recovery from alcoholism or drugs, a job for someone unskilled or with a prison record, a place to stay that did not cost much, friendship that would overlook smells and bad social skills, boundaries, tough love—the list was long.

One night in late spring, I felt desolate. I could not see what God was doing and even wondered if God really cared. The needs were so great, and we had so little. Even those who made one step forward in progress often fell two steps back in the process. I drove to our Wednesday night Bible study but did not go in. Instead, I walked around the panhandle of Golden Gate Park. As dusk set in, I was lost in despairing thoughts berating God for not helping more and begging for some guidance about what to do, when someone called my name.

It was Ernie. We called him Snow. Everyone did. Later, I learned that he had gotten his nickname from the drug he had peddled as a young man. He had decided to get sober, and we had helped him find one of the precious few spaces in a rehab center. He had just left the Bible study and was headed to the bus stop when he spotted me. He had to be back before dark, or they would lock him out. I offered him a ride.

We drove to the south side of the city, a not-so-nice area where rehab centers usually exist for the poor. As he got out, Snow hesitated, then stuck his head back in the car. He said: "You know, I wouldn't be here if you hadn't kept saying hi to me and calling me by name when I was a drunk sleeping in the church's driveway. You told me you'd pray for me, and I believe that you did. Thank you."

He left, and I drove home in tears. I had been listening to the rant of despair that said: *Why are you wasting your life on people like this? Why is this world so cruel? Why does the city spend its money on a new stadium when thousands are sleeping on the streets? Where is God? Why doesn't God do something to alleviate all this pain? Why do the churches bolt their doors and call the police when someone wants to find nighttime shelter beneath the steps?*

Snow was my answer to all those questions. His quiet voice reminded me that I was being Spirit-led in the wilds of the city. Right before me was a word from God, if I would but stop and listen.

Jesus' call to his disciples was to follow him. We are not required to understand all that we are asked to do. We are not shown the final outcome to all of our efforts. It is in the following that faith is forged. Where we are led matters less that the One we are following.

Reflecting and Recording

1. Have you ever been led by the Spirit to go somewhere or to perform some act of kindness for someone? What happened?

2. Are you open to spiritual nudges? How do you recognize the prompting of the Holy Spirit?

3. How do our relationships with other followers of Jesus affect our ability to be faithful to the way of Jesus? Can you be a person of faith without being involved in the work of Christ in the world?

DAY TWO: CALLED TO JOIN IN

The first chapters of Luke identify Jesus as the long-awaited Redeemer and show us how his identity as the Beloved one of God is revealed and tested. Luke now turns to Jesus' public ministry.

Jesus preached his first sermon, called the disciples, and began to teach and heal throughout the region of Galilee. This section of the Gospel shows how Jesus began to live out his mission. Jesus traveled from town to town balancing his time between teaching and healing. All the while, he made a priority those who were outsiders to the common understanding of who merits a place in the family of God. As he went from place to place, more people began to follow him, including lepers, women, and Gentiles. Having such a following led to opposition, especially from the religious authorities. The cost of following Jesus became clear: Jesus came to call all people to a new identity that is not based on ethnic origins or family relationships. The identity of a follower of Jesus is rooted in an understanding of who Jesus is, and having this identity requires participation in his mission. Anyone who seeks to follow Jesus will face difficulties and rejection, too.

Spend your remaining time today reading Luke 4:14–5:11; 7:1–9:51. If time allows, read all of Chapters 4–9. It is a worthy goal to read through the entire Gospel during the course of this study. However, the focus of this week's daily readings and the group session will be on the specific passages.

Reflecting and Recording

1. Why did the townspeople of Nazareth become so angry at Jesus' first sermon? Does it sound like a radical sermon to you? Why or why not?

2. What image of Jesus do you form from reading these passages? If you had heard him preach and had seen him heal, what kind of response do you think you might have had to him?

3. How would you summarize the mission of Jesus after reading these passages?

DAY THREE: LEARN, THEN DO AS JESUS DID

The public ministry of Jesus began with a hometown sermon that did not end well. Jesus declared that he was the fulfillment of the scriptural promise of liberation. He pointed to himself as the one anointed to declare that the poor—that is, anyone outside the boundaries of society's wealth and support—were now included; that release from the captivity of sin, illness, and rejection was possible; and that the time of God's reign on earth had come with all of its promise of economic and political relief from the oppressive practices of the current system. This is a radical promise, and his first hearers could not believe that a local boy had said such things.

Jesus left home and continued to preach and heal in other villages. Soon Jesus called the first disciples, and they accompanied him as his companions. (Chapter 6, verse12 tells us that Jesus spent the night in prayer before he named the Twelve, whom he designated as apostles, his authorized representatives.) Their first task was simply to be with Jesus and to be instructed by him. They were to listen and follow him, even when they did not understand; and the gospel shows that they often puzzled over Jesus. In time, they would be sent out in shared mission—to do what Jesus did; but in the beginning, they were to spend time with Jesus, learn from him, and little by little to understand who Jesus was and what he had come to do. Then, they could go and do likewise.

It took the disciples a long time to understand who Jesus was. In Luke 9:18, we find Jesus praying alone with the disciples nearby. He asked them who the crowds thought he was. Many thought he was like the prophets they had heard of before. Then Jesus asked them, "Who do you say that I am?" Peter had come to understand that Jesus was the Messiah—the long-awaited one who had come to save and release people from sin and oppression. Peter's answer showed that he finally understood who Jesus is and what he had come to do. It had taken him a while. He had witnessed many miracles and listened to many lessons; and eventually he recognized the core identity of the one he had chosen to follow.

Reflecting and Recording

1. Why do you think the disciples had to learn by watching Jesus rather than just by being handed an instruction sheet? How does learning by imitating another person differ from book learning?

2. Jesus set the example of praying before selecting his followers and making large decisions. Do you pray before making large decisions? If so, what has been the result? If you don't do this, try it.

3. Who do you say Jesus is? List phrases that describe who Jesus is to you.

DAY FOUR: HAVE COMPASSION

Repeatedly during Jesus' Galilean ministry we see Jesus heal people, and almost always those whom he heals are those who are ostracized or deemed unworthy in the larger community. The story of the raising of the widow's son at Nain in Chapter 7, beginning with verse 11, is such an example. This story takes place, archeologists believe, about 35 miles from Nazareth.

Luke begins this story with the words: "As he approached the gate of the town, a man who had died was being carried out. He was his mother's only son; and she was a widow." To Luke's first hearers, this was a clue. This story sounds familiar. In fact it sounds very much like the story of Elijah and the widow of Zarephath in 1 Kings 17, which ended with a resurrected life.

So when Jesus visited the village of Nain and saw the grieving widow and the funeral processional, he stopped it right then and there. While the hearers of the gospel may have suspected that Luke's retelling of this event would have predicted its ending, the widow could not have known that she would not bury her son that day. The Scripture text says, "When the Lord saw her, he had compassion for her and said to her, 'Do not weep.' "

Compassion literally means "to suffer with another person." The Hebrew word paints a picture of having one's intestines move with feelings of pity and sadness and a desire for action. Jesus saw a widow in grief and was moved with compassion. The very word for *widow* in Hebrew means "to be unable to speak." As was the custom, a widow without husband or son was someone who had no one to speak on her behalf. Jesus recognized this woman was all alone with few if any provisions and no voice to speak or no one to care for her. The first thing Jesus did was see her plight and feel her pain himself.

Read what Jesus did next: He walked right up to the stretcher and touched death directly. He made physical contact with the widow's son. (A Jewish rabbi like Jesus by ritual law was not to touch anything dead.) Yet, compassion moved him to action—to touch the untouchable, to hug the sad and lonely, to come close to the sick and dying.

Then Jesus did the most amazing thing. He spoke new life into the dead. He said, "Rise! Get up. Go to your mother."

In the simplest of terms Jesus saw someone who had been abandoned and was in need. And he was moved with compassion. He then walked right into the sadness and grief and touched death directly. He summoned life to return to what had been dead. Elijah prayed in First Kings, "O LORD my God, let this child's life come into him again" (verse 17:21). Jesus simply said, "Young man, I say to you rise!" In both instances, God brought new life where death reigned. The young man was restored to life; and the widow, who would have had no place in the society without a husband or son to provide for her and give her a place to live, now had a way to belong and thrive.

This story and many others in Luke show that indeed Jesus' mission was to release those who were captive by social stigma, economic problems, or oppressive political laws and let them live again in the company of others.

Reflecting and Recording

1. What moves you to compassion? When was the last time you experienced a physical sense of compassion for someone else?

2. How willing are you to walk into a situation where someone is suffering or grieving? Would you go if it were clear to you that you were called to act on someone else's behalf? Is it ever best just to stay out of a situation when another is in pain? How can you tell when you are to act and when you are not to act?

3. Jesus was willing to cross boundaries. What boundaries are you willing to cross? Are you comfortable crossing racial, economic, or ethnic boundaries? Is this ever a part of following Jesus?

DAY FIVE: WHEN TO ACT

Years ago, I learned the physical feeling of compassion the hard way. I traveled with a few friends and my husband to Calcutta, India. I had worked with the homeless but was still totally unprepared for the street crowds, the foul smells, and the legions of bone-thin beggars. The humid weather and contaminated water made us all sick with dysentery. Most of our group came to give care but instead spent the weeks in bed. Those of us who were left standing dragged ourselves, sick and weak, to Howrah Shishu Bavan orphanage to volunteer. We walked through narrow dirt roads in a shanty town until we reached a simple cement structure. Once inside we were swarmed by five- and six-year-olds; but a line of a half-dozen dark-eyed babies propped up on the floor caught my attention. One face captivated me. My heart lurched, my stomach rumbled; and this time it was not because of the water. He seemed different, sadder. His arm was like a twig; and as I got closer and saw well-formed teeth through his gaping mouth, I realized with full force—a full punch to my stomach—that this was no baby. He weighed no more than ten pounds, but he had to be much older. I reached down and scooped him up, and he clung to me like a scrawny bird. He did not laugh or smile. The only expression I saw was a look of agony as I laid him on his back so one of the Indian caretakers could pour some sticky-looking medicine down his throat.

At lunchtime Jackie, another in our group, fed this boy. After two heaping bowlfuls he still wanted more. I asked one of the workers about this child and discovered he'd been left the day before by parents who could no longer feed him.

He was terrified, bereft; and when I finished for the day, I felt such sadness. His plight weighed on me. I knew he would never starve under the care of the Missionaries of Charity. He would slowly physically come back to life, but what about the whole of his life?

I felt so confused. Why did God give me the capacity to feel compassion for this child and not give me an equal ability to make things better for him in the long run? Jesus had raised the widow's son from the dead and restored him to his mother. What could I do?

Later that night while writing in my journal, I reread these words of Mahatma Gandhi:

> When in doubt and confusion about your next step, think of the poorest, most wretched [person] you know. Then think if your next step will serve to enhance dignity and give [that person] back some control of his [or her life]. Then the doubt and confusion will disappear. You will know your next step.
>
> (On a statue of Gandhi, New Delhi airport)

I don't know what happened to that little boy in Calcutta. I trust new life found him as his physical health was restored. I do know that when I came home, a friend of mine took in a foster child with HIV/AIDS. When I first met him, his brown skin, dark eyes, and emaciated form reminded me of that little boy in Calcutta. I could not help that boy, but I could commit to helping Patrick and his mom. For the next six years, I witnessed the rebirth of both a child who had lost mother and father and the building of a new family around a child who had none. I saw resurrection power before my very eyes. Jesus' example of compassion sets the standard for us. When we see someone in great need, we must act to help give her or him back some measure of control or dignity. That is what Jesus requires of his disciples both in the first century and today.

Reflecting and Recording

1. What situations in the world make you feel hopeless? What problems seem beyond a solution?

2. Who is the "poorest, most wretched" person you know? (Don't overlook someone who is in your own extended family.) What could allow this person to regain some measure of dignity?

3. What specific acts of compassion is the Lord requiring of you? Perhaps your Sisters group can take action to alleviate someone's suffering.

DAY SIX: A PSALM OF THANKSGIVING

Read Psalm 40, a psalm of thanksgiving for deliverance from illness and sin. This is the prayer offered from a thankful heart. This writer has known past hardship and has waited with patience for deliverance from illness, sin, and shame. Now in a time of trouble, she is willing to trust that God will again provide help and hope. This is a prayer any of us who have known the goodness of the Lord can pray wholeheartedly.

DAY SEVEN: GROUP MEETING

Prepare for the meeting in quiet, restful activities. Think about what you have learned and what you would like to share. Remember your group members in prayer and prepare yourself to hear what they have to say as well as what God is saying to you.

Week Four:
A Journey of Faithfulness

DAY ONE: MAKING PROMISES AT THE TABLE

Readings for the Week: Luke 10–11:19; Psalm 116

Years ago, a work-related project took me to the home of a woman of Middle Eastern descent. Her uncle, a renowned Bible scholar, had left her, his heir, his treasure: a centuries-old parchment manuscript of the Bible that was handwritten in Aramaic, the language Jesus spoke. Her uncle had spent his lifetime writing commentaries and translations of the Bible that helped unpack the original metaphors and idioms of the everyday language Jesus spoke.

This woman wanted help in finding a library or museum that would preserve the rare book and care for it for centuries more.

At first we talked, as those discussing business do. We traded facts and opinions and rehearsed possible avenues of action to pursue. After the conversation was completed, my boss and I prepared to leave when she beckoned us into her kitchen.

"Sit," she motioned to chairs by her kitchen table. "We must eat together. In the custom of my people, if you eat with me, then I know you will not betray me."

She took a plate of dolma (grape leaves stuffed with rice), then added a basket of savory flatbread, a bowl of almonds picked from her orchard, and dried figs and dates; she poured goblets of fruit juice and placed the food and drink before us.

She took her place at the table and bid us to eat. We did, looking straight into one another's eyes. That experience taught me the sacramental nature of hospitality. Something is sacramental when ordinary gifts, like bread and wine, become a visible sign of grace. We ate together saying little because words were not necessary. Each of us knew that we were not just sharing a meal; we were making a promise to respect and care for one another in the days to come.

Throughout Jesus' journey toward Jerusalem, he sat and ate with his friends and taught them another way of living. He called them to true discipleship, sharing his very life with them.

Reflecting and Recording

1. What has been entrusted to you? How are you making sure that it is preserved for the future?

2. What makes eating together more than merely sharing food? Why is table fellowship so important to Christian community and building trust?

3. How do the cultural differences between Jesus' time and ours have an impact on our understanding and living out of the gospel?

DAY TWO: A NEW ALLEGIANCE

In our study last week, Jesus called the disciples who joined him in his early public ministry in Galilee. This week's Scripture passages describe Jesus and his disciples as they turn the sights of their ministry toward Jerusalem—the location of the Temple, which was the sacred heart of what we know as "second-Temple" Judaism. (In the Old Testament the first Temple was built by Solomon and destroyed by the Babylonians in 586 B.C. The Temple known as the second Temple was rebuilt on the same site 70 years later and stood until several decades after the death of Christ. Jesus was a second-Temple Jew.)

Luke is foreshadowing trouble for Jesus. We see that Jesus' message of forgiveness, healing, and inclusion of all, based on the condition of the heart rather than on one's ethnic background or economic status, begins to rankle some listeners. Throughout Chapters 10–21, not only are the religious leaders turning against Jesus but also some in the crowds. Luke is slowly showing how Jesus must face suffering and rejection to fulfill his divine message. We begin to understand that there are those who reject Jesus' teachings and wish to silence him.

During the journey to Jerusalem, the disciples learned that following Jesus was different and more difficult than they had first thought it might be. They consistently had difficulty understanding Jesus' indirect teaching and parables. Jesus answered questions in a way that made the disciples (and make us) think differently and harder about the demands of the gospel. For instance, Jesus told the story of the good Samaritan in response to a lawyer who wanted to inherit eternal life. The lawyer clearly expected Jesus to give him a list of demands. Instead Jesus told a story that showed that the one who does what God requires must realign allegiances and eliminate preconceived notions of acceptable behavior. One must be willing to help those who may have been thought of as untouchable or outside of one's concern. This is not an easy life Jesus requires.

Repeatedly, Jesus emphasized that hearing the word of God was to be followed by living out the word. The kingdom of God was coming to pass as Jesus and his followers followed God's ways regardless of whether doing so made them popular or led them down a path of suffering. The journey to Jerusalem is the journey of obedience.

Spend the rest of your time today reading Luke 10–11:9. If you can, read the entire section (9:51–19:48) that describes the journey to Jerusalem. This long section of Scripture is filled with many familiar and wonderful stories. There is great value in seeing how an entire book of the Bible reads from beginning to end. If you make it a priority to read each section of Scripture, you will have mined the depths of the Gospel of Luke in six short weeks.

Reflecting and Recording

1. From the Scripture reading in Luke 10–11:9, how would you summarize the mission Jesus has asked his followers to share with him?

2. What for you is the most challenging part of Jesus' instructions to his disciples in this passage?

3. What actions are pleasing to Jesus in these passages? What attitudes or beliefs are challenged?

DAY THREE: SHARE YOUR LIFE

Hospitality, both offering and receiving it, is key to understanding Jesus' journey to Jerusalem. Jesus instructed the disciples to be on the lookout for the welcome they would receive. The welcome that was extended by the villagers the disciples met was linked to the welcome of the message of the gospel itself. Said another way, Jesus shows us that belief and actions are linked. It is impossible to choose to accept the message without also accepting the messenger.

The parable of the good Shepherd tells us that the definition of one's neighbor is broader than we might expect, and that the love of one's neighbor flows from the love of God. Remember that just before the story was told, the lawyer recited the law that sums up the way to inherit eternal life: "You shall love the Lord your God with all your heart, and with all your soul, and with all your strength, and with all your mind; and your neighbor as yourself" (Luke 10:27). The lawyer was right. Jesus said, "You have given the right answer; do this, and you will live" (verse 28). The lawyer may have been hoping that the definition of who was his neighbor was manageable. Jesus assured him that it is not.

Right after Jesus finished talking with the lawyer and admonished him to "go and do likewise" by showing mercy to those in need, Luke launches into another well-known story—the story of Mary and Martha. While this story often is told emphasizing Mary's listening pose as a better response to Jesus than Martha's busy, bustling style, the core concerns of the story actually revolve around showing us how to offer hospitality and welcome to Jesus.

Jesus traveled toward Jerusalem. He and his followers needed food, rest, and friendship. Jesus and the disciples probably dropped in on the two women looking for all three. However, what Jesus wanted above all and received from Mary was her attention. He wanted her to come close to and be transformed by an encounter with him. Throughout the Gospel of Luke those who listened to the word and responded to it are those who became Jesus' disciples. Mary, by listening to Jesus' teaching and putting herself in a pose to heed his words, exhibited the necessary traits of a follower of Jesus. Martha's service was not what Jesus rebuked; instead, it was her worry and distraction. Jesus told her that hospitality is not just about food or facilities but about the love and attention shown to the one who has come to share your life.

Hospitality can be defined as the friendship offered to a visitor. The word *host* or *hostess* originally meant "a lover of strangers." In biblical times, hotels did not exist. Sojourners, like Jesus and his disciples, depended upon those living along the route for provision and protection. Jesus needed the hospitality of Mary and Martha, but Jesus made it plain that they needed even more to hear and heed the word he brought and lived.

Reflecting and Recording

1. Write your own definition of *hospitality.* What does it mean to you to be a "lover of strangers"?

2. If Jesus or one of his disciples came to your home unannounced, what kind of welcome would they find?

3. How do you show attention to Jesus in a way that allows him to share your life?

DAY FOUR: FIRST THINGS FIRST IN PRAYER

After Jesus showed that those who are disciples are those who hear and heed the message he brings, Luke immediately turned to Jesus teaching the disciples how to pray. What we often refer to as the Lord's Prayer is more aptly described as the "Disciples Prayer."

First, this section in Luke 11:1-4 makes it clear that Jesus is a person of prayer. You may have noticed during your reading of Luke that Jesus regularly retreated to a quiet place to pray, often during the night. Yet, when Jesus was asked to teach his disciples to pray, he did not offer a lengthy description of how to spend hours in prayer. Instead, Jesus suggested a short prayer that could be prayed regularly and often.

The prayer begins by calling God "our Father." The passage that immediately follows the Lord's Prayer lets us know that the Father to whom we pray will provide for us and will not trick us by giving us something harmful like a scorpion when we ask for an egg. We are to approach God as a parent capable of friendship to those in need and desirous of offering good gifts to his children.

When approaching this good Father, we are to "hallow his name." In ancient cultures one's name was equivalent to one's character. "To hallow God's name" means simply to trust and revere the full character of God.

As God's disciples, when we pray, we are to begin by keeping first things first. Praying for God's kingdom to come is paramount. That is the first order of the disciple's agenda. Then, we are to pray for present needs like bread, help with past sins that require God's forgiveness, and protection against future trials. What a great way to pray! This prayer covers all of life from the profound to the practical, from the past to the present and into the future.

Reflecting and Recording

1. Jesus lived a life that had a rhythm of prayer followed by action. How are prayer and action connected in your life?

2. When you pray, what do you call God? What are the character traits you ascribe to the one you address in prayer?

3. Write your own prayer that follows the pattern of the Disciple's Prayer: Begin with reverencing God, then praying for the coming of God's kingdom, for your basic needs, for help with past sins, and for protection from future trials.

DAY FIVE: FAITH HAS NO CHECKLIST

Have you ever wanted to ask Jesus this question: "So what exactly is it that you want from me?" I have.

Sometimes the demands of being a friend of Jesus and a follower of his teachings seem too hard and complex. Like the lawyer who asked Jesus, "What must I do to inherit eternal life?" I sometimes would prefer a clear checklist of things to do and not to do.

Scripture assures us that Jesus is never going to give any of us a simple punch list because we are being called to a life of faith, not just to a lifestyle of good deeds. Jesus sends us out to declare God's peace in the world even in places where we will not find welcome. We are given the hard and often thankless task of loving hard-to-love people and sharing our goods with those we would rather ignore. We are asked to put aside our busy and necessary tasks to pay attention to Jesus and his teaching as we bask in his nearness. We are instructed to pray knowing that God hears our prayers and wants us to seek and ask for what we need.

A common thread that runs through all of these instructions and demands is that we do none of them alone. We go out and come back again in Jesus' name. We love others because we love the Lord, our God, with heart, mind, and soul. We pray knowing that the One who loves us, listens to us, and cares for us also hears our prayers. The common thread is a relationship. The life of faith we are called to live is based on a vital and ongoing connection between our lives and God's love. Faithful love can never be reduced to a punch list or scorecard. We know what Jesus wants from us only as we stay close enough to live day by day within the sound of his voice and the reach of his spirit. We are called to live our faith in relationship with Jesus.

Reflecting and Recording

1. What specifically do you believe God wants from your life right now?

2. How do you stay close enough to Jesus to hear his voice and sense his spirit? Is this easy or hard for you?

3. Every relationship has a beginning point and some high and low points. What is the state of your relationship with Jesus right now?

DAY SIX: A PSALM OF GRACIOUS CARE

Read Psalm 116, a psalm that focuses on God's past gracious acts of care. The writer knows God has heard and heeded prior requests and can trust that God's character and actions will remain steady in the future. This psalm traces one person's spiritual journey of trial and thanksgiving. These words express a deep fidelity between God and the one who serves God over many years. This prayer affirms that not only is God's message of love reliable, so also is God's character.

DAY SEVEN: GROUP MEETING

Prepare for the meeting in quiet, restful activities. Think about what you have learned and what you would like to share. Remember your group members in prayer and prepare yourself to hear what they have to say as well as what God is saying to you.

Week Five:
God's Unfailing Love
in Dark Times

DAY ONE: THE WAIT FOR NEW LIFE

Readings for the Week: Luke 22–23; Psalm 118

One Good Friday my family traveled to the Natural History Museum in Manhattan. Our youngest daughter had brought home a publicity flyer about a butterfly exhibit, and we were enchanted with the thought of walking through a simulated rain forest as myriads of multicolored butterflies flitted from flower to plant.

In a hallway leading to the glass-covered butterfly sanctuary, we stopped to look at the vast butterfly collection housed on shelves against a wall. I examined a spectacular black-and-blue specimen. How could such delicacy and detail be rendered on a wing that was powder thin? How could such a fragile creature survive in rain-soaked forests full of natural predators?

I marveled at the butterfly, pressing my nose to the glass and tracing its shape with my finger. As I did, a chill crawled up my back like a small furry thing. This beautiful creature before me was dead, carefully pinned down. Its life had been sacrificed so that people like me could learn and benefit from it; its vital quickening of life was gone. Sadness washed over me, and I couldn't determine why. After all, as a child, I'd pinned many water bugs and spiders to foam board for school insect collections. Then I realized that the butterfly was shaped like a cross. Its wings were pinned horizontally, its body inert against the board. It looked crucified.

Soon, it was our turn to walk through the rotating doors and into the hot air of the butterfly sanctuary. The butterflies looked like bits of colorful ribbon landing on the waxy leaves. A brown plain-Jane variety landed in my husband's hair. When it opened its wings, this creature with an ordinary exterior showed off the shimmering underside of its lavender wings.

After a while, we gathered by the pupa cage. Two brown twiglike cocoons were throbbing and twisting, ready to burst with new life. Slowly, a slimy inch-long wet mass discarded its now-useless shell and hung quietly. The attendant told us to come back in 20 minutes to see how it was gathering strength and unfurling its wings, readying itself for flight.

After a long solitary struggle in the darkness of transformation where it had waited and followed the unspoken wisdom built into its very being, the butterfly would live. My spirit, joined in the butterfly's transformation, took wing. This was how it should be.

Jesus, the beautiful one, was crucified, nailed to wood and left to die. A long, desolate wait followed. Life seemed over, and sadness reigned. But in God's good time, Jesus returned, all light and glory, and our spirits were raised with him.

Reflecting and Recording

1. Transformation often takes time and happens in dark places. What transformation are you waiting for in your own life?

2. How do you deal with suffering? Do difficulties or pain turn you toward or away from your faith?

3. How does the cruxifiction of Jesus help or hinder you in understanding Jesus' unfailing love for you?

DAY TWO: HAVE FAITH IN THE ONE YOU KNOW

The section we studied last week recounts Jesus' journey to Jerusalem. With each step and encounter along the way, the tension mounts. We know something awful is about to happen. In the very first pages of Luke, Simon prophesied to Mary, "This child is destined for the falling and the rising of many in Israel, and to be a sign that will be opposed so that the inner thoughts of many will be revealed—and a sword will pierce your own soul too" (2:34-35). Those prophetic words were now coming true: division between people was rampant. Beginning with Chapter 22 the conflicts that had been building now turn into accusations and betrayals. The chief priest was looking for a way to put Jesus to death. Satan overtook Judas, and the disciples squabbled about who was the greatest. Even after they ate a covenant-sealing meal with Jesus, they could not honor Jesus' request to stay awake and pray with him during his great night of suffering prayer.

This section of Luke shows us that in a time of testing, people's loyalties are challenged, their deepest beliefs are questioned, and behaviors they never considered in the realm of possibility are enacted. This section of Luke also shows that the way to remain true to God's will in a time of trial is through earnest, submissive prayer. Following God may mean suffering of the highest order. Friends may betray us; enemies may accuse us; and we may beg for God to open another way. In all these things Jesus shows us that God's way is not easy but we travel it accompanied by

God's presence. Others may fall away, but God will attend our every step.

Jesus' own life reveals that God's unfailing love is present even in our deepest experiences of suffering and doubt. Jesus' life also reveals that there are times when it seems nearly impossible to see any evidence of God's goodness and graciousness. In those terrible times, we are called to follow as Jesus did, trusting in our relationship with our good and powerful God who has proven faithful in the past. Faith is not about knowing the end result but about trusting in the character of God and God's promises that have proven faithful over time and through many trials.

Spend the rest of your time today reading Luke 22–23. This section of Luke is among the most familiar. We are reminded of these chapters each time Communion is served in our churches. We read the section through often, especially at Easter. These chapters form the heart of the Christian faith. Don't presume, however, that because it is familiar, you might skip the reading. Please take time to read this section aloud. Although only a few pages in length, it describes the events that lie at the suffering heart of the Christian faith. Walk the long road to Calvary with Jesus just as the early disciples, imperfect as they were, did. See anew the definition of obedient, self-giving love.

Reflecting and Recording

1. With whom do you most identify in these chapters of Luke? Judas, another of the disciples, Peter, one of the arresting soldiers, one of the religious leaders, Pilate, Barabbas, one of the criminals, or one of the Galilean women? Why?

2. In a time of great trial what most would challenge your loyalties to Christ? Fear of punishment? Ridicule? Abandonment? Pain?

3. In this saddest of times, where do we still see God's unfailing love? Who are God's faithful followers through it all?

DAY THREE: A BOND OF FIDELITY AND LOVE

When Jesus and his disciples gathered in the upper room, it was not just food he intended to share. Jesus had asked his disciples to prepare both the place and the meal. He wanted to share and declare a new understanding of the Passover meal with those closest to him.

The Passover meal took place during a festival period when many Jews would converge on Jerusalem to celebrate their identity as a people freed and redeemed by God. All those present would have shared an understanding of the purpose and elements of the meal. Unleavened bread was a reminder of the haste with which they had left Egypt. The cup signified blessing and thanksgiving for the special relationship between God and God's people. Jesus intended to give new meaning to these ancient symbols.

Jesus took, blessed, broke, and gave the disciples bread saying, "This is my body, which is given for you." To give one's body for another is to lay down one's life for one's friends. Jesus was showing the disciples in no uncertain terms that his life would be offered for them. His impending sacrifice wasn't just a result of the will of his enemies, it was also a gift to those he most loved.

Jesus then took the cup saying that it signified a new covenant between them. A *covenant* is a relational word that points to a bond of fidelity and love. Jesus was declaring his unfailing love for his disciples, those who would be his representatives on earth when he was gone, even when he knew that those he loved so completely would not stand with him when he needed them most.

He served them food and said, "Remember me." The act of remembering, which Jesus requested, was not that of simple recall. He was asking more than to be fondly remembered or nostalgically revered as a past teacher. Jesus was asking them to "re-member," to "re-put-together" his body by their actions. They were to remember Jesus by becoming his body and by prolonging his mission to bring good news to the poor and proclaim the year of God's favor. This remembering called for action motivated by God's unfailing love.

Jesus also knew that his disciples would be able to remember him each time they broke bread and drank wine together. Just as a family remembers the love of a family member whose influence remains even after death, the disciples could savor Jesus' nearness and feed on his love. We can too. The Lord's Supper is not just a memory of a special meal. It is a means of God's unfailing love to nourish us body and soul.

Reflecting and Recording

1. Different churches have different understandings of what the Lord's Supper signifies. What do you understand this sacrament to mean? How does it allow you to experience the unfailing love of Jesus Christ?

2. The new covenant initiated by the Last Supper Jesus had with his disciples created a bond of faithfulness and love between them. Jesus made this covenant even though the disciples were not perfect in their ability to follow him. Can a covenant remain even among partners who fail? How so?

3. Do you understand Jesus' death on the cross as a sacrifice demanded by his enemies or as a gift of love for his followers? Or perhaps you have a different view. What is it?

DAY FOUR: FOR THE SAKE OF LOVE

Jesus was a man of prayer. We learn that as his life was threatened and his friends began to fight and fall away, he "went, as was his custom, to the Mount of Olives" to pray. This mountaintop prayer time is the watershed moment in the Gospel of Luke. It is the moment when we wait to see if this Jesus who had come in fulfillment of ancient prophecies as the Messiah would really follow God no matter what. The ending of the story hinges on this moment. Will Jesus turn away and refuse to go one step more; or will Jesus step out in obedience, no matter the cost to him? Will he become the servant of all, even unto death; or will he choose instead to be the powerful, strong, militant messiah for whom the crowds are crying out? Whose will is going to prevail? Will God's will or the will of God's people be done? The all-important moment of decision was settled in prayer.

As he struggled with this life-and-death decision, Jesus asked his friends, his followers, to pray with him; specifically, he asked them to pray that they not come into temptation or trial. He warned them that they would be tested and tried and might want to turn away from God's purpose when it seemed unreasonable and unbearably hard.

In a pose of submission, kneeling and alone, he prayed for God's will to be done, and an angel appeared to him to give him strength. Angels had come to Zechariah and to Mary to help them understand how what seemed impossible could be done. An angel appeared to Jesus, too, as he prayed until his body bled. Already he was shedding his blood in obedience to God.

Within a short span of time, Jesus was betrayed; and one of his disciples struck out with his sword and cut off the right ear of the high priest's slave. His disciples were ready to protect and defend their powerful, strong, and militant Messiah; but Jesus healed the man's ear and said, "No more of this!" His path was clear. He was to be the servant Messiah who conquered not through might or power but through suffering for the sake of love.

Has anyone ever suffered for you? Parents often suffer for their children. Spouses often suffer for each other over years spent together. Many of us would choose to suffer for those we love when necessary, and that suffering can forge great bonds of love and gratitude. But Jesus has suffered for his friends, strangers, and those not yet born.

Reflecting and Recording

1. Could your life be described as a life of prayer? What have you learned from the example of Christ about the place and importance of prayer?

2. What happens when you pray, "Not my will but yours be done"? Are you willing to pray this prayer? Why or why not?

3. If someone suffers for you, how does it affect your relationship? How do you feel toward someone who has willingly put aside her or his personal comfort or safety for you? How does Jesus' sacrifice show you his unfailing love?

DAY FIVE: THE UNEXPECTED RECIPIENTS OF LOVE

It is remarkable to realize that not one of Jesus' disciples is mentioned in Chapter 23. Jesus went alone before Pilate, then Herod, and back to Pilate again. A man named Simon of Cyrene picked up Jesus' cross and carried it up the hill. An unknown person was asked to bear the cross; his disciples, who were so quick with the sword on the Mount of Olives, were nowhere to be found.

The disciples had disappeared, no doubt out of fear and perhaps out of ignorance (they still seemed to misunderstand the kind of messiah Jesus was born to be). Most teachers would turn away from students who just did not seem to be learning the basic truths. But Jesus kept on teaching his message of unfailing love and open welcome to the end of his life. Imagine how Jesus' last words sounded both to those who knew him well and to those who misunderstood him and cruelly called for him to die. Jesus' final words were words of unimaginable goodness: "Father, forgive them; for they do not know what they are doing." No matter what others had done or not done for him, whether his message was fully understood or completely disregarded, Jesus provided a way back to the heart of God. He offered forgiveness to the end.

Jesus died suspended and in agony between criminals and strangers. Jesus' last human exchange was with a criminal who recognized him and that his kingdom was not one of earthly power. This criminal realized that Jesus' kingdom was one of love that is willing to go all the way to death for those who do not deserve such love. Because he understood who Jesus was and why he had come, Jesus in turn promised, "Truly I tell you, today you will be with me in Paradise."

Even for this criminal, all it took was the recognition of who Jesus is, and the doors of eternity swung wide. No one was given special privileges for spending long years walking and learning with Jesus. All are given entrance to eternity who recognize who Jesus is and ask to be remembered by the suffering Messiah. Those who have loved him long and those who love him late are equally promised Paradise. In God's social system, all are welcomed through faith.

Reflecting and Recording

1. Are you like one of the disciples who followed Jesus for many years, or more like one who recognized Jesus at the last moment? Why does Jesus offer Paradise both to last-minute converts and long-term disciples? Is this a fair way to offer love and forgiveness?

2. What kind of faith does the criminal dying next to Jesus exemplify? Why would Jesus promise that he would be with him in Paradise?

3. Forgiveness and the promise of Paradise are linked in this passage. How does forgiveness open people to receiving Paradise both now and in the future?

DAY SIX: A PSALM OF REDEEMING LOVE

Read Psalm 118, a psalm often quoted in the New Testament as a reference to the rejection of Christ and his steadfast love that outlives even his cruel death on the cross. Verse 5 can be prayed as a prayer similar to the one the criminal prayed on the cross: "Out of my distress I called to the LORD, / the LORD answered me and set me in a broad place." The psalm reminds us that what is rejected by the world is redeemed and rewarded by God when we turn to God for help.

DAY SEVEN: GROUP MEETING

Prepare for the meeting in quiet, restful activities. Think about what you have learned and what you would like to share. Remember your group members in prayer and prepare yourself to hear what they have to say as well as what God is saying to you.

Week Six:
Hope Does Not
Disappoint Us

DAY ONE: ALL CAN BE WELL

Readings for the Week: Luke 24; Psalm 103

On a beautiful sunny late afternoon in October of 1989, the earth shook. I was in my room at a conference center just a handful of miles from the epicenter of the Loma Prieta earthquake when the lamp began to sway. I headed first for the open glass patio door, then remembered that the safer place was beneath the door frame.

The moving lasted several long terrifying seconds that seemed to pass in slow motion. The whole world seemed upended. When things again stood still, I ventured outside to the parking lot where dozens of people gathered around a radio that was tuned to the World Series. As we listened, the earth began to shake some 60 miles north of us in San Francisco. The mighty, unseen movement of the earth was snaking its way up the California coastline.

For three days we couldn't go home. The road that led from the Santa Cruz mountains to San Francisco was closed due to mudslides. The radio was our lifeline. We heard stories of fires and of a bridge collapse that left dozens dead. When I finally reached home, I was grateful that a little time spent sweeping up broken glass and painting and plastering ceiling cracks was all I would need to set my personal space aright.

My private world was safe, but all around me chaos still reigned. I stayed glued to the television, waiting for more news. The news showed broken and burnt buildings, smashed cars, more injuries, and impossible mounds of rubble to sort and sift and clear. Hope often seemed distant. The heroic efforts of hundreds of rescue workers held hope though. Finally, some good news flashed across the screen. A man had been found alive in the Cypress Freeway collapse. Rescuers had thought it improbable that anyone had survived, but this man had.

Tears formed in my eyes, and I cried in joy for this man I had never met. Hope was alive. This man's survival did not take away the rubble or rebuild people's lives; but it did point to the truth that, even in terrible circumstances, all can be well. Good can rise from rubble; God can shine a light even in the darkest despair and bring hope.

Reflecting and Recording

1. How do you define *hope?*

2. When have you experienced hope in a time of despair? What did the experience teach you?

3. What makes some people trust God in terrible times and others turn away? What is your basic tendency?

DAY TWO: JESUS IS WALKING BESIDE YOU

We have paged through the life of Jesus according to Luke. We have read of how he was a long-expected child, chosen by God to be his Beloved Child, destined to preach and announce good news to the poor. We have seen how he ministered with others and healed those on the margins of society. We have watched as crowds flocked around him and how they soon began to turn away. Conflict has been rife in these stories of Jesus, and eventually this "division in Israel" that was predicted by Simeon has led to Jesus' torture and death. We could easily stop reading the story here and believe that it is simply another classic tragedy, where the hero was thwarted and a good person died young.

But thanks be to God, Luke's story of Jesus does not end here. There is a final chapter. Chapter 24 of Luke focuses on answering the questions: How can we understand what has happened to Jesus? How can the death of this one sent to redeem all the world turn out to be exactly what was needed when it looked like the end of all hope? Luke helps us answer these questions by showing us that we are blind to the mysterious truths about Jesus until our eyes are opened to his presence. When we realize that Jesus is walking close beside us, when we pay attention to the times when our hearts are burning within us, then we will begin to accept that we are witnesses to the wondrous work of Jesus by faith.

Spend the rest of your study time today reading the last chapter of the Gospel of Luke. Pay special attention to the emotions and experiences of the disciples as they try to understand the amazing end to the story.

Reflecting and Recording

1. How do you understand what happened to Jesus? What truths have been revealed during the past weeks you have spent studying the Gospel of Luke?

2. How can the death of this one sent to redeem all the world turn out to be exactly what was needed when it looked like the end of all hope?

3. Have you ever sensed the presence of Jesus in your life? How did you know what was taking place?

DAY THREE: THE UNEXPECTED PATH TO LIFE

The women who went early to the tomb were not traveling with hope. They were grief-stricken, numb, angry, and despairing. Their dearly beloved teacher and friend was dead and buried. Yet, when they arrived at the tomb and found it empty (a hopeful sign for those who wanted nothing more than for Jesus to be alive), their first response was not rejoicing but perplexity. When the women told the apostles, they discounted it as an "idle story," nothing more than wishful thinking. Even someone who had lived and walked with Jesus like Peter, who ran to the tomb to see for himself that it was empty, could not easily believe that something so extraordinary, so far beyond his expectations, could really be true. Grief and despair blinded even those closest to Jesus; they could not imagine the possibility that hope could live through the tragedy of all time.

Immediately after describing the Resurrection Luke tells another journey story. Cleopas and his friend were on their way to Emmaus. As they walked, they tried to make sense of all that had happened to Jesus. We know they were so sad that they didn't even recognize Jesus in their midst. Their perception of events prevented their response of faith and recognition. Instead they simply retold their sad story to the familiar stranger. (Isn't it true that people in pain often need to tell and retell their story of pain many times before it is possible to see any other interpretation or possible outcome?)

Jesus' response to their discussion was to shake his head and call them foolish. Then, he recast this story of tragedy against the backdrop of what the prophets had foretold in Scripture. Perhaps he pointed them to Isaiah 53:4-5:

> Surely he has borne our infirmities
>   and carried our diseases,
> yet we accounted him stricken,
>   struck down by God, and afflicted.
> But he was wounded for our transgressions,
>   crushed for our iniquities;
> upon him was the punishment that made us whole,
>   and by his bruises are we healed.

He reminded them that the story of Jesus cannot be interpreted or understood without the bigger story of God's redemptive love. Jesus was still trying to help them understand that he did not come to be their expected Messiah; he came to be the one sent by God to redeem Israel and open wide the doors to redemption for all. God's topsy-turvy kingdom operates with a different set of rules: *the first shall be last, the last shall be first, and a suffering servant rather than a conquering king shall be able to vanquish death and be raised to new life and offer hope to all who follow him.*

The two on the road to Emmaus still did not understand Jesus' teaching. It took Jesus entering into their home and breaking bread for them to see that it was the same Jesus who had said to his disciples while breaking bread, "This is my body, which is given for you." Only then did their despair vanish and their hearts confirm, "It is he! He is alive!"

Henri Nouwen writes, "Despair is our inner conviction that, in the end, it is utterly impossible to stop anything from coming to nothing" (*Jesus: A Gospel,* Orbis, 2001; page 122).

When despair takes hold, our eyes can only see that our expectations have been dashed, our hearts have been broken, our futures turned into dust.

Jesus shows us that the way to liberation and love may be through the worst that could happen. The most tragic and pain-filled times of your life may be the path to new life. When we turn our eyes away from our version of the story, we begin to see the bewildering story of our lives as well as Christ's through the eyes of God's great gift of hope.

Reflecting and Recording

1. What has kept you from recognizing Jesus in your life?

2. Can the worst that has happened to us turn into the way to liberation?

3. How do you think Christ's version of the events of your suffering differs from your version? How would Christ's loving eye describe your life?

DAY FOUR: BEARERS OF CHRIST'S LOVE

The Gospel of Luke opens with the story of Jewish extended family being chosen to prepare for and bear the long-promised Messiah. The Gospel of Luke ends with Jesus surrounded by his disciples, those who will be his witnesses, the bearers of his legacy of faith.

Faith ties supercede family ties in Jesus' life. In Chapter 8 of Luke, Jesus redefined his family as those who follow God. Mary, his mother, is not mentioned again by name. From other Gospels we know that she traveled with Jesus; she traveled among those who followed him. We can be fairly certain that she was among the "women beating their breasts and wailing" mentioned in Luke 23, those who followed Jesus as he carried his heavy cross up the hill. The Gospel of John records the last words Jesus said to his mother. Near death, he said, "Woman, here is your son." And to the beloved disciple, "Here is your mother" (John 19:26-27). Jesus, a source of connection and comfort until the end, brought together these two people whom he loved so they would not be alone in their grief.

In Luke's description of the death of Jesus, we read that "all his acquaintances, including the women who had followed him from Galilee, stood at a distance, watching these things" (23:49). Mary probably prayed to be anywhere else when Jesus was trudging to Golgotha, but still she stayed with him. I imagine she looked to the heavens and prayed prayers full of anguished questions and despair. But still she stayed close. Mary would have watched as Jesus was nailed to the cross, stood by as his clothes were divided up like war spoils, and listened as he promised eternity to one of the criminals who hung by his side. She would have seen him breathe his last breath and commend his spirit into God's hands. She would have watched him be taken to the tomb.

Mary kept returning to Jesus' side, even unto death, when all of her dreams died, and her trust was betrayed. After all, the angel had called her "Favored One." How could she feel favored when this one she carried, loved, and followed died a terrible death?

Then, in her faithfulness she perceived God's plan unfold in the last place few would believe anything holy could happen. First there was death and doubt. Then, hope won out.

Reflecting and Recording

1. What does Mary's example show you about the importance of standing firm in faith even when terrible things take place?

2. Have you witnessed God at work bringing hope and restoration in your life and in the lives of those you love even in times of trial and grief?

3. What have you witnessed of Christ's suffering in your life? What can you share with another about Jesus' favor toward you?

DAY FIVE: WITNESSES TO UNFAILING LOVE

Throughout most of the Gospel of Luke, Jesus was in the company of his disciples. He called them, traveled with them, served and healed with them, prayed with them, sent them out to be his ambassadors, ate with them, and shook his head at their slowness to comprehend who he really is.

In the very last scene of this Gospel, Jesus called his followers "witnesses." These were the ones who had been present during his ministry, death, and resurrection. Now they would witness his final blessing and ascension. These were the despairing ones who are now joyful and strong.

Jesus gave them a new identity. Witnesses are those who have seen something for themselves and can testify to this truth by telling others. But Jesus told them that they must wait to witness until they had received the empowerment and leading of the Holy Spirit.

Not only is this wise advice (certainly, it is best to speak to others about Jesus when the Spirit leads and provides the words), it is also a foreshadowing of what is to come. The Gospel of Luke is the first part of a two-part series. The Book of Acts is the second part, the part that begins with the outpouring of the Spirit and the nativity of the Christian church.

The story is not yet over. Acts picks up where Luke leaves off and fills in the details of how a Jewish messiah became the savior of the Jew, Greek, slave, free, male, and female, and made all people one in Christ Jesus. And where the Book of Acts leaves off, *we* begin. We, too, are

Christ's witnesses. Those who have had our hearts burn within us also have stood in Christ's presence as friends.

Reflecting and Recording

1. What does it mean to you to wait to speak to others until the Holy Spirit leads?

2. How are you like the early disciples? How are you different in the way you might bear witness to Jesus' life?

3. Describe the friendship you now have with Jesus after spending six weeks learning more about his unfailing love. What kind of friend is Jesus to you?

DAY SIX: A PSALM OF UNIVERSAL PRAISE

Spend your final few moments of this study praying Psalm 103. This psalm is both a personal witness to God's gracious and steadfast love, compassion, and redemption as well as a psalm of universal praise. The angels and hosts of heaven join in the praise. All creation joins in to "bless the LORD, O my soul, / and all that is within me, / bless his holy name."

DAY SEVEN: GROUP MEETING

Prepare for the meeting in quiet, restful activities. Think about what you have learned and what you would like to share. Remember your group members in prayer and prepare yourself to hear what they have to say as well as what God is saying to you.

This is the last meeting for your group using this study. You may have already talked about the possibility of continuing to meet. Now is the time to finalize those plans. Whatever you choose to do, be deliberate about determining a timeline in order to facilitate a clear commitment from group members. As a group designate one or two persons to follow through with whatever decisions are made.

Your sharing during this session should reflect on the entire six-week experience. Begin with your workbook experience this past week, but save enough time to discuss your overall six-week experience.

For Further Reading

Borg, Marcus. *Meeting Jesus Again for the First Time*
HarperSanFrancisco, 1995.
   A New Testament scholar summarizes recent scholarship on the historical Jesus and its relationship to personal faith.

Green, Joel B. *The Gospel of Luke: The New International Commentary on the New Testament*
Grand Rapids: Eerdmans, 1997.
   This commentary combines insight on the first-century Roman world with a narrative understanding of the persuasive purposes of the gospel.

Nouwen, Henri J.M. *The Heart of Henri Nouwen: His Words of Blessing*
Edited by Rebecca Laird and Michael Christensen.
New York: Crossroads, 2003.
   A collection of the most inspiring passages from Nouwen's books interspersed with biographical essays on his life.

Nouwen, Henri J.M. *The Inner Voice of Love: A Journey Through Anguish to Freedom*
New York: Doubleday, 1996.
   Through short "spiritual imperatives" Nouwen probes the availability of God's love in times of anguish.

Nouwen, Henri J.M. *Jesus: A Gospel,* edited with an introduction by Michael O'Laughlin.
Maryknoll: Orbis Books, 2001.
   A retracing of Jesus' major life events as interpreted by Henri Nouwen's writings, illustrated by paintings and sketches by Rembrandt.

Nouwen, Henri J.M. *Life of the Beloved: Spiritual Living in a Secular World*
New York: Crossroads, 1992.
   Henri Nouwen, a Catholic priest, explains to his friend, a secular journalist, what it means to live a spiritual life.

Peterson, Eugene. *Praying with the Psalms: A Year of Daily Prayers and Reflections on the Words of David*
HarperSanFrancisco, 1993.
   Eugene Peterson walks readers through a year of psalms offering reflections seasoned by his many years as a pastor and devoted follower of Christ.

Pohl, Christine D. *Making Room: Recovering Hospitality as a Christian Tradition*
Grand Rapids: Eerdmans, 1999.
   This highly readable and helpful book traces the history and importance of hospitality as a central act of faith throughout various eras of the Christian tradition.

Yancey, Philip. *The Jesus I Never Knew*
Grand Rapids: Zondervan, 1995.
   A respected Christian journalist takes a look at the Jesus found in the gospels and peels back the sentimentality often attached to Jesus to reveal a challenging, compassionate, and unpredictable Jesus.